# Feeling Scared

by Rosalyn Clark

BUMBA BOOKS™

LERNER PUBLICATIONS ◆ MINNEAPOLIS

**Note to Educators:**

Throughout this book, you'll find critical thinking questions. These can be used to engage young readers in thinking critically about the topic and in using the text and photos to do so.

Lerner Publications Company
A division of Lerner Publishing Group, Inc.
241 First Avenue North
Minneapolis, MN 55401 USA

For reading levels and more information, look up this title at www.lernerbooks.com.

**Library of Congress Cataloging-in-Publication Data**

Names: Clark, Rosalyn, 1990–
Title: Feeling scared / by Rosalyn Clark.
Description: Minneapolis : Lerner Publications, c2017. | Series: Bumba books. Feelings matter | Audience: Age 4–7. |
    Audience: K to grade 3. | Includes bibliographical references and index.
Identifiers: LCCN 2017002405 (print) | LCCN 2017013817 (ebook) | ISBN 9781512450286 (eb pdf) | ISBN 9781512433692 (lb :
    alk. paper) | ISBN 9781512455489 (pb : alk. paper)
Subjects: LCSH: Fear in children—Juvenile literature. | Fear—Juvenile literature.
Classification: LCC BF723.F4 (ebook) | LCC BF723.F4 C53 2017 (print) | DDC 155.4/1246—dc23
LC record available at https://lccn.loc.gov/2017002405

Manufactured in the United States of America
1 – CG – 7/15/17

Expand learning beyond the printed book. Download free, complementary educational resources for this book from our website, www.lerneresource.com.

# Table of
# Contents

# Feeling Scared

Scared is a feeling.

When do you feel scared?

Maybe you are in

a big crowd.

You are afraid of getting lost.

Why else
might a big
crowd make
you afraid?

Maybe it is your first day

at a new school.

Meeting new people can be scary.

Maybe you had

a bad dream.

Sometimes people dream

about their fears.

**What is something scary a person might dream about?**

Maybe you climbed the ropes

at the park.

You were up very high.

This made you feel scared.

Many people have the same fears.

Do you get scared in the dark?

Your friend might be afraid

of the dark too.

When you are scared,

your heart beats fast.

You may want to run and hide.

Try taking deep breaths.

Are you afraid to

do something?

Ask a friend to

come with you.

Your friend can help

you stay calm.

It is okay to feel scared.

Talk to friends or family

about your fears.

Telling someone about it can help.

**Who do you talk to when you feel scared?**

# Picture Quiz

Which child is scared? Point to that picture.

# Picture Glossary

**calm**

not angry
or excited

**crowd**

a large group
of people

**fears**

things that
scare you

**feeling**

an emotion or
thought

# Read More

Butterfield, Moira. *Scared!* London: QED Publishing, 2016.

Kawa, Katie. *I Feel Scared.* New York: Gareth Stevens, 2013.

Parr, Todd. *The I'm Not Scared Book.* New York: Little, Brown, 2011.

# Index

## Photo Credits